P9-AQF-028

Silent Kay
and the
Dragon

Written by Larry Dane Brimner
Illustrated by Bob McMahon

Children's Press®
A Division of Scholastic Inc.
New York • Toronto • London • Auckland • Sydney
Mexico City • New Delhi • Hong Kong
Danbury, Connecticut

To Carson and Cassidy Brimner.
—L. B. D.

To Tyler: May you grow up to be as smart and brave as Silent Kay.
—B. M.

Reading Consultant

Cecilia Minden-Cupp, PhD
Former Director of the Language and Literacy Program
Harvard Graduate School of Education
Cambridge, Massachusetts

Cover Design: The Design Lab
Interior Design: Herman Adler

Library of Congress Cataloging-in-Publication Data

Brimner, Larry Dane.
  Silent Kay and the dragon / by Larry Dane Brimner; illustrated by Bob
McMahon ; reading consultant, Cecilia Minden-Cupp.
     p. cm. — (A rookie reader: silent letters)
  ISBN-13: 978-0-531-17546-0 (lib. bdg.)   978-0-531-17783-9 (pbk.)
  ISBN-10: 0-531-17546-4 (lib. bdg.)   0-531-17783-1 (pbk.)
  1. English language—Consonants—Juvenile literature. I. McMahon,
Bob, 1956– , ill. II. Title. III. Series.
  PE1159.B75 2007
  428.1'3—dc22   2006024390

I knew a knight named Silent Kay.

She battled a dragon one bright day.

But it seemed that poor Kay forgot . . .

Her laces were knitted into a knot!

Kay was brave.
Kay was bold.

But, alas, she tripped.

She sailed.

She rolled.

Kay couldn't stop. WHEEEEEE!

She grabbed the dragon's knobby knee.

Kay said to the dragon,
"Please excuse me."

The dragon kneeled.
"Of course. Care for tea?"

"I'd love to, but I wish I knew
just how I could unknot my shoes!"

"We dragons are known for our fire, our fight. But we're also good with knots that are tight."

So, this story just goes to show
how much dragons really do know!

Word list (82 words)

(Words in **bold** have the silent *k* sound.)

a	dragon's	**knee**	of	story
alas	excuse	**kneeled**	one	tea
also	fight	**knew**	our	that
are	fire	**knight**	please	the
battled	for	**knitted**	poor	this
bold	forgot	**knobby**	really	tight
brave	goes	**knot**	rolled	to
bright	good	**knots**	said	tripped
but	grabbed	**know**	sailed	**unknot**
care	her	**known**	seemed	was
could	how	laces	she	we
couldn't	I	love	shoes	were
course	I'd	me	show	we're
day	into	much	silent	wheeeee
do	it	my	so	wish
dragon	just	named	stop	with
dragons	Kay			

About the Author

Larry Dane Brimner taught school for twenty years. He now writes full-time for children from his home office in Tucson, Arizona, where he only occasionally battles dragons and Gila monsters. Among his many titles for Children's Press are *How Many Ants, Firehouse Sal, A Flag for All*, and *Butterflies and Moths*.

About the Illustrator

Bob McMahon lives in sunny Southern California with his wife, Lalane, daughter, Tyler, and their crazy dog Riley.